MAKING MUSIC

Written by
Bernadette
Parkhurst-Smith

THE SCIENCE OF BRASS INSTRUMENTS

KidHaven
PUBLISHING

Published in 2027 by
KidHaven Publishing, an Imprint of Greenhaven Publishing, LLC
2544 Clinton St., Buffalo, NY 14224

Written by: Bernadette Parkhurst-Smith
Edited by: Rebecca Phillips-Bartlett
Designed by: Ker Ker Lee

All facts, statistics, web addresses, and URLs in this book were verified as valid and accurate at time of writing. No responsibility for any changes to external websites or references can be accepted by either the author or publisher.

Cataloging-in-Publication Data

Names: Parkhurst-Smith, Bernadette.
Title: The science of brass instruments / Bernadette Parkhurst-Smith.
Description: Buffalo, NY : KidHaven Publishing, 2027. | Series: Making music | Includes glossary and index.
Identifiers: ISBN 9781534570191 (pbk.) | ISBN 9781534570207 (library bound) | ISBN 9781534570214 (ebook)
Subjects: LCSH: Brass instruments--Juvenile literature.
Classification: LCC ML933.P375 2027 | DDC 788.919--dc23

Printed in China

CPSIA compliance information: Batch #QS27KH: For further information contact Greenhaven Publishing LLC at 1-844-317-7404.

Please visit our website, www.greenhavenpublishing.com.
For a free color catalog of all our high-quality books, call toll free 1-844-317-7404 or fax 1-844-317-7405.

Find us on

Photo Credits – Images courtesy of Shutterstock.com, unless otherwise stated.

Cover & Recurring – RidiUmbrella, hatsak, AnnaStills. 2–3 – Malikova Nina. 4–5 – alphaspirit.it, SpeedKingz. 6–7 – Gearstd, VisualArtStudio. 8–9 – MUKHORTOV OLEKSANDR, Michae Allen. 10–11 – the palms, Monkey Business Images. 12–13 – mollyrosey, Orhan Cam. 14–15 – Bryan Littel, Debra Anderson. 16–17 – Mr.Note19, Tack-Ma. 18–19 – Igal Vaisman, ChameleonsEye. 20–21 – lego 19861111, Ivan Yohan. 22–23 – Jack R Perry Photography, Malikova Nina.

CONTENTS

Words that look like <u>this</u> can be found in the glossary on page 24.

SOUND MEETS SCIENCE

If you have heard a musical instrument, it might seem a little like magic. How do instruments make beautiful music, instead of everyday noises? It is not magic. It is science!

Let's learn about what happens when we play musical instruments.

This book is all about brass instruments. These instruments are played by buzzing your lips into a mouthpiece. Most instruments in this group are made of a type of metal alloy called brass.

This is a brass band. Each person is playing a brass instrument.

WHAT IS A SOUND?

A sound is a vibration. A vibration is when something moves back and forth really quickly. Vibrations travel through the air, like waves in the sea. When ears feel these vibrations, they hear a sound.

As sound moves through the air, it is called a sound wave.

For brass instruments, you make the vibration by buzzing your lips into the mouthpiece. This sends vibrations through the air inside the instrument. The sound that comes out is called a note.

Let's find out how different brass instruments make different sounds.

TROMBONE

A trombone is a brass instrument. It has a part called a slide. This is a bent tube that can be moved in and out to become longer or shorter.

Trombones are made of metal.

The slide helps change the pitch of the note. Making the slide longer means the air can vibrate more slowly, which makes a lower-pitched note. A shorter slide means quicker vibrations, which makes a higher-pitched note.

TUBA

When you blow into a tuba, the air travels through a long, bendy tube and out the other end. A tuba has buttons called valves that you press to change the pitch.

A tuba usually has three or four valves, but some have more.

When you press a valve, it opens up more space for the air to travel down. This is a way of making the tubes longer. Longer tubes mean slower vibrations, which lowers the pitch.

The tuba can make lower notes than most other brass instruments.

FRENCH HORN

A French horn also has valves to create different notes. It looks very different because of its circular shape. Like other brass instruments, the part where the sound comes out is called the bell.

Sometimes this instrument is just called a horn.

Horns are usually held by putting your right hand inside the bell. The shape of the bell helps the sound waves come out of the instrument and reach your ears.

SOUSAPHONE

A sousaphone is a large, loud instrument. It often plays the lower notes in a marching band. It wraps around you so that you can walk around while playing. It usually has three valves.

This is a marching band with sousaphone players.

A sousaphone has a big bell. The bigger the bell, the further the sound will travel. This is because the sound waves can travel out of the instrument more easily. This makes the sound louder.

A sousaphone's bell points toward the listener, which also makes it louder.

TRUMPET

A trumpet is a smaller brass instrument. It usually has three valves. Smaller instruments often mean quicker vibrations and a higher pitch. This means trumpet players can play very high notes.

Trumpets are usually made of metal, but some are made of plastic.

A mute is a piece that is put into the bell. Trumpet mutes come in many shapes and sizes. Practice mutes make the trumpet quieter by stopping sound waves from coming out of the bell.

Mutes can also change the type of sound a trumpet makes.

DIDGERIDOO

A didgeridoo is a long instrument made of wood. It might not look like a brass instrument, but it is played by buzzing your lips into one end. This means it is sometimes grouped with brass instruments.

Didgeridoos are from Australia.

A didgeridoo plays one low note. You can change the sound by changing your mouth shape. There is a special way of breathing to play without stopping. This lets the note last for a long time.

Aboriginal Australians play the didgeridoo as a way of feeling closer to nature.

THE SERPENT

The serpent is a very old instrument. It is made of wood and played by buzzing your lips into the mouthpiece. It is a big instrument, so it can play low notes.

The serpent gets its name because it looks like a snake.

Instead of valves, the serpent has six finger holes. By covering the holes with your fingers, you are changing the length of the tube that the air travels down. This changes the pitch.

BUGLE

A bugle has no valves or slide. It can make different notes based on how fast your lips buzz. Bugles have been used in history to send messages on a hunt or in battles.

Bugles have to be loud for the messages to be heard.

It is time to start practicing! To play a brass instrument, you make a tight buzzing sound with your lips, almost like an elephant sound. Which brass instrument would you like to play?

Can you make a buzzing sound with your lips?

GLOSSARY

Aboriginal Australians groups of people who have always lived on the continent of Australia

alloy something made from mixing two or more metals

battles fights between two armies

hunt a chase to catch an animal

marching band a group of musicians who play brass and woodwind instruments while walking to a set pace

mouthpiece the part of an instrument you blow air into

pitch how high or low a musical note is

INDEX